TULSA CITY-COUNTY LIBRARY

MXJC
6/17 ST
AL

D1199304

SCIENCE AT WORK

LIGHT

AT

WORK

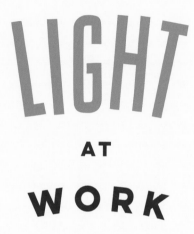

LAUREN KUKLA

Consulting Editor, Diane Craig, M.A./Reading Specialist

Sandcastle

An Imprint of Abdo Publishing
abdopublishing.com

abdopublishing.com

Published by Abdo Publishing, a division of ABDO, PO Box 398166, Minneapolis, Minnesota 55439. Copyright © 2017 by Abdo Consulting Group, Inc. International copyrights reserved in all countries. No part of this book may be reproduced in any form without written permission from the publisher. SandCastle™ is a trademark and logo of Abdo Publishing.

Printed in the United States of America, North Mankato, Minnesota

062016
092016

THIS BOOK CONTAINS
RECYCLED MATERIALS

Design: Mighty Media, Inc.
Content Developer: Nancy Tuminelly
Production: Mighty Media, Inc.
Editor: Liz Salzmann
Photo Credits: Shutterstock, Wikimedia Commons

Library of Congress Cataloging-in-Publication Data

Names: Kukla, Lauren, author.
Title: Light at work / Lauren Kukla ; consulting editor, Diane Craig, M.A./reading specialist.
Description: Minneapolis, Minnesota : Abdo Publishing, [2017] | Series: Science at work
Identifiers: LCCN 2016000311 (print) | LCCN 2016010746 (ebook) | ISBN 9781680781410 (print) | ISBN 9781680775846 (ebook)
Subjects: LCSH: Light--Juvenile literature.
Classification: LCC QC360 .K85 2017 (print) | LCC QC360 (ebook) | DDC 535--dc23
LC record available at http://lccn.loc.gov/2016000311

SandCastle™ Level: Fluent

SandCastle™ books are created by a team of professional educators, reading specialists, and content developers around five essential components—phonemic awareness, phonics, vocabulary, text comprehension, and fluency—to assist young readers as they develop reading skills and strategies and increase their general knowledge. All books are written, reviewed, and leveled for guided reading, early reading intervention, and Accelerated Reader™ programs for use in shared, guided, and independent reading and writing activities to support a balanced approach to literacy instruction. The SandCastle™ series has four levels that correspond to early literacy development. The levels are provided to help teachers and parents select appropriate books for young readers.

EMERGING · BEGINNING · TRANSITIONAL · FLUENT

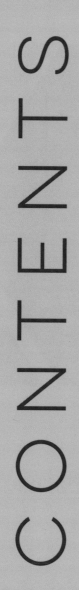

CONTENTS

ABOUT LIGHT

Have you ever turned on a flashlight?
Or watched a rainbow?

You were seeing light at work!

Light is very important. It helps plants grow. Sunlight keeps Earth warm.

Light lets us see the world we live in.

Light is a kind of **energy**.

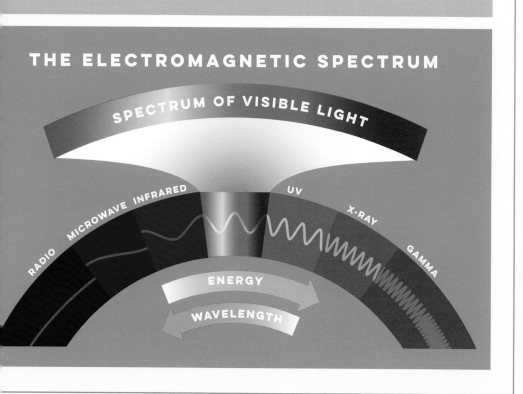

This **energy** is called **electromagnetic radiation**. We see part of it as light.

Nick reads a book. He uses light.
But what is light made of?

Albert Einstein was a scientist.
He studied light. Einstein learned

that light is made up of small **bundles** of **energy**. These are called photons.

Photons move very fast. Light is
the fastest thing in the **universe**.

It takes sunlight eight minutes to reach Earth.

Light travels in a straight line. But what if an object is in the way?

Sometimes the light passes through it. Or light may bend around it.

Light may **reflect** off an object. This happens when Sara looks in a **mirror**.

Objects can also **absorb** light.
Black objects absorb the most light.

Sunlight has every color in it.
Its light hits an apple.

Most colors are **absorbed**. Red is **reflected**. This is the color you see.

THINK ABOUT IT

Look around you! Where else is light at work? How do you use it?

GLOSSARY

absorb – to soak up.

bundle – a group of things that are together.

electromagnetic radiation – waves of energy related to electricity and magnetism.

energy – a natural power that can affect other things.

mirror – a polished or smooth surface, such as glass, that reflects images.

reflect – to throw or bounce back after hitting a surface.

universe – all matter and space in existence.